G000049603

PRAYERS FC

Compiled by

Jean M. Scott
New Revised

**Messenger Publications,
37 Lower Leeson Street,
Dublin 2.**

Published by
Messenger Publications,
37, Lower Leeson Street,
Dublin 2.
Tel: 676 7491. Fax: 661 1606.

With ecclesiastical permission,
Dublin 1997.

ISBN 1 872245 50 1

PREFACE

The variety of the prayers in this little anthology may alert you to human needs and encourage you to lift up your mind and heart to God. For it is prayer that keeps the soul fresh and renews the world. In prayer human trust and divine liberality meet.

Friend, should this little booklet help you to pray, do not forget a prayer for its compiler and for all who helped in bringing it to you.

Prayer

Some prayer may be an unknown path,
Explored when racked by fear,
Or weed-grown lane men stumble down,
When danger hovers near.
But prayer should be a shining road,
A highway smooth and broad,
Which Christians journey day by day,
In closer walks with God.

Gail Brook Burket

A Daily Offering of Masses

O merciful God, I humbly beg a share in all the holy Masses that will be offered and all the holy Communions that will be made from the rising sun till the going down thereof: for myself and all those who are dear to me, for all who pray for me, for all who may have injured me or whom I may have injured: for my dear parents, relatives and benefactors: for all who may be delayed in Purgatory through my fault; for the Holy Souls for whom our Blessed Lady and St Joseph desire help: for those in Purgatory who during life were especially devoted to the Adorable Sacrament, to the Precious Blood, to the Sacred Heart, or to the bitter passion and death of our divine Lord; for the poor, the sick, the afflicted in body, for all who are grievously tempted, for all who are suffering crosses either spiritual or temporal; for those in their last agony, for the poor obdurate sinners, and those who have none to pray for them; for the just that they may receive the crowning grace of final perseverance; and, finally, for all religious communities.

Prayer for the Church

O Holy Spirit, Creator, mercifully assist your Catholic Church and by your heavenly power strengthen and establish her against the assaults of all her enemies, and by your love and grace renew the spirit of your servants whom you have anointed, that in you they may glorify the Father and his only-begotten Son, Jesus Christ our Lord. Amen.

Prayer for Church Unity

'That they may all one, even as we are one, I in them and thou in me, that they may become perfectly one, so that the world may know that thou has sent me' *John 17:21*.

O God, who makes straight the crooked and gathers what is scattered and guards what is gathered, mercifully pour forth over the Christian people the grace of your union, that they may shun division, and, uniting themselves to the true pastors of your Church, may find strength worthily to serve you.

Prayer for Nuns

Dear Lord, take under your very special care these your consecrated virgins, that they may toil and pray unceasingly for their brethren. Wherever they are, in silent cloister, in school, hospital, mission land, or other apostolate, let them feel, dear Lord, especially in their hour of trial, the immense power of your love for them.

Teach us also to know the tremendous value of their consecrated lives in your sight, and to appreciate the selfless work they do for us.

Dear Lord, whose own gentle Mother is the Queen of Virgins, stay close to these her special daughters when they feel forsaken and misunderstood. When their many hidden sacrifices seem so fruitless, whisper in their hearts, Lord, that pure virgin souls like theirs are the delight of your sacred heart, and give them strength and grace to persevere until you call them to their special place among your elect in everlasting glory. Amen.

Prayer for the Missions

Lord, make me an apostle of your faith,
Where there is the darkness of paganism,
let me spread light.
Where there is the hate of Communism, love;
Where there is the error of heresy, truth;
Where there is the frustration of sin, forgiveness;
Where there are Moslems, devotion to Mary.
Grant that by my prayers and alms I may give to each continent what it requires;

To Africa, a native clergy of black hands lifting white hosts;

To Asia, a rich harvest from the red blood, seed of her martyrs;

To Oceania, a necklace of Islands made into a Rosary for the faith;

To Europe, already so tired, a renewal of youth at the altar of God;

To America, an exchange of material riches for the pearl of great price.

Let me send my offerings where I cannot go:

My pains to comfort sufferers whom I will never see;

And my sacrifices to help plant the Cross in lands that know not yet of the Crucified;

I ask this through Christ our Lord. Amen.

Increase of Vocations to the Priesthood and Religious State

O God, who does not desire the death of the sinner, but rather that he be converted and live, grant, through the intercession of Blessed Mary, ever Virgin, and of all the saints, an increase of labourers for your Church, who, co-operating with Christ may give themselves for the salvation of souls through the same Jesus Christ, your Son, our Lord, who lives and reigns with you in the unity

of the Holy Spirit, world without end. Amen.
Mary, Queen of the clergy, pray for us; obtain for us a great number of holy priests.
O Lord, bless your Church with holy priests and fervent religious.

The Aspirant

When I was just a little tot,
So often would I go
Around to Church and whisper sweet:
'Dear Lord, I love you so
In just a few years more, my King,
If it's your will for me,
I'll lay aside my pretty things
And come your spouse to be'.
Now, as I humbly kneel within
His convent-chapel shrine,
He whispers to me soft and low:
'You came! and now you're mine'.

The Nun

Two hands to do a thousand earthly things
For him, her only one, the King of Kings.
Two hands to scrub or sweep, to mend all day,
And yet be quick and eloquent to pray.
Two hands to guide and teach his little tots;
To feed and bathe, and tuck them in their little cots.

Two hands to nurse the sick, to help the blind
And do whatever else is good and kind.
Two eyes to light with rapture at His name;
And lips that ask no more than it to frame.
All inward-glowing beauty - so well earned!
Which comes with knowing wondrous love
returned!

Tom Freegard Kelly

Prayer for Seminarians

O Jesus, eternal High Priest, I offer you, through
your immaculate mother Mary, your own precious blood, in all the Masses throughout the
world, as a petition for all seminarians, your
future priests. Give them humility, meekness, pru-
dence and a burning zeal for souls. Fill their
hearts with the gifts of the Holy Spirit. Teach
them to know and love the Church, that they may
always and everywhere speak, act and think with
her, the glorious Spouse of Christ. Teach them
generosity and detachment from the passing
things of this world; but, above all, teach them to
know you and to love you, the one and only eternal Priest. O good Shepherd of souls, hear this my
prayer for all our seminarians.

Prayer for Priests

O Jesus, eternal Priest, keep Your priests within the shelter of your sacred heart, where none may touch them. Keep unstained their anointed hands, which daily touch your sacred body. Keep unsullied their lips, daily purpled with your precious blood. Keep pure and unearthly their hearts sealed with the sublime marks of the priesthood. Let your holy love surround them and shield them from the world's contagion. Bless their labours with abundant fruit, and may the souls to whom they minister be their joy and consolation here, and their everlasting crown hereafter. Amen.

Prayer for one's Confessor
(or any other priest)

Give him, Lord, eyes to behold the truth,
A seeing sense that knows the eternal right,
A heart with pity filled and gentlest truth,
A manly faith that makes all darkness light.
Give him the power to labour for mankind,
Make him the mouth of such as cannot speak;
Eyes let him be to groping men and blind;
A conscience to the base; and to the weak
Let him be hands and feet; and to the foolish, mind;
And lead still further on such as your Kingdom seek.

For the Bishop

Grant, O Lord, to your servant our Bishop, that, by preaching and doing such things as are right, he may by the example of good works edify the minds of those under his authority, and receive from you, most tender Shepherd, an everlasting recompense and reward.

Amen.

For the Pope

O Jesus, eternal High Priest, we, the millions of believers, humbly beg you to preserve, defend and save our Holy Father, your Vicar on earth, for many years. Be with him always dear Lord, to lighten the burden of his tremendous task. Whether he weeps or rejoices, whether he hopes or offers himself as a victim of charity for his people, we desire to be united with him; we desire that the cry of our hearts should be made one with his. All that he asks of you this day, we too ask it of you in union with him. Bless him dear Lord, and each and every one of us who delight in being members of his flock under the eternal Good Shepherd.

Amen

Prayer for the Young

To us all things are new, dear Lord, so new
And shining fair, as though they had not been
Until we came to find them, we begin
In wonder plucking flowers fresh with dew
As though there were no autumn. And the blue
Limitless sky seems ours this little while
That we are young. And all things share a smile
With us alone. The world is ours to do
With what we will. For these we thank you, Lord.
For all things bright and gleaming, all things rare,
For love and life and dreams. Lord, let them be
Ageless for always, somehow, somewhere stored
So we can find them. And this is our prayer:
When we are old, give us their memory

Thomas J Horan Jr.

Prayer for Youth

Be with them as they try to grope their way
Through all the baffling mazes of today:
Assure them they will find it if they but seek,
Give strength when indecision makes them weak;
Encourage them whenever faith ebbs low,
Set in their minds the dauntless will to grow;
Be patient with their fumbling toward a goal;

Gird their impulsiveness with self-control
Encircle them with love as with a host,
When they deserve it least and need it most.
Let love of you, with its consuming fire,
Burn from their hearts the dross of base desire.
Fill them with discontent, until they see
There is no lasting joy apart from thee.
Grant them no peace until their lives fulfil
Their full design, according to your will.

Gail Brook Burket

A Student's Prayer

Under your protection, dearest Mother, and under the invocation of your immaculate conception, I wish to pursue my studies; and I declare that I study chiefly from this motive, that I may be the better able to assist in spreading God's glory and your worship.

I beseech you, therefore, most loving Mother, Seat of Wisdom, to favour and assist my work, and whatever success I may obtain, I promise on my part, as is but just, to attribute it all to your intercession with God.

Amen.

Our Lady of Good Studies, pray for us.

A Teacher's Prayer

You, O Lord, are my strength, my patience, my light and my counsel. For my own conduct and for that of my pupils, grant me the spirit of wisdom and understanding, the spirit of counsel and fortitude, the spirit of knowledge and piety, the spirit of holy fear of you, and an ardent zeal to procure your glory. I unite my labours to those of Jesus Christ, and beg the most blessed Virgin, St Joseph, the Guardian Angels and St John Baptist de la Salle to protect and guide me in this holy work.

A Nurse's Prayer

O my God, I am about to begin the day's work. Teach me to receive the sick in your name. Give to my efforts success, sweet Jesus, for the glory of your holy name. It is your work: without you I cannot succeed. Grant that the sick whom you have placed in my care may be abundantly blessed, and not one of them be lost because of anything that is lacking in me. Help me to overcome every temporal weakness and strengthen in me whatever may enable me to bring the sunshine of joy to the lives that are gathered round me day by day. Make me beautiful within for the sake of your sick ones and of those who will be influenced by them. Amen.

A Doctor's Prayer

Dear Lord, healer of men's bodies and souls, I kneel before you. Since every good and perfect gift must come from you, I pray:

Give skill to my hand, clear vision to my mind, kindness and sympathy to my heart. Give me singleness of purpose, strength to lighten at least a part of the burden of my suffering fellowmen and a true realization of the privilege that is mine. Take from my heart all guile and worldliness that with the simple faith of a child I may rely always on you.

Amen.

A Lawyer's Prayer

O Lord, supreme ruler and judge of our hearts, who reads and judges with perfect justice even our most secret thoughts, help me as a lawyer to do my utmost to carry charity and justice in my every dealing with my fellow men. Help me to judge others as you would have me judge them, even as I would wish to be judged by you, when I shall stand before you, my Creator and Judge, to receive the just reward of my actions.

Amen.

A Musician's Prayer

Dear Lord, who are praised and glorified by even the smallest action performed for your greater honour and glory, accept, we beseech you, the homage we seek to render you, by offering our music as an act of love and worship to you. May it rise to Heaven as a hymn of praise to mingle with the music of the heavenly choirs, and may we, by your grace dear Lord, be able to join them one day, in singing your mercies for ever. Amen.

For the Apostolate of the Press

O glorious St Paul, apostle of the gentiles, who with zeal busied yourself in destroying at Ephesus those books which you knew well would have perverted the minds of the faithful: turn your eyes upon us also at this present day. You see how an unbelieving and liberal press is attempting to rob our hearts of the precious treasure of faith and Christian morals. Enlighten, O holy apostle, the minds of so many misguided writers, that they may cease once for all to do harm to souls with their evil doctrines and lying insinuations. Move their hearts to hate the evil that they have done and are doing to the followers of Jesus Christ. Obtain for all journalists the strength and grace to publish what they know to be right and true; and for us also, obtain the grace of being ever docile to the voice of our Holy Father that so we may never allow ourselves to indulge in the reading of evil books, but may seek instead to read and to spread those books which by their sound doctrine shall assist all of us to promote the greater glory of God, the spread of his Church and the salvation of souls. Amen.

Lay Apostles' Prayer

Lord Jesus, you have called us to make our humble contribution to the work of the hierarchical apostolate; you have asked your heavenly Father not to remove us from the world but to preserve us from evil. Grant us an abundance of your light and your grace that we may crush in ourselves the spirit of darkness and sin, so that, aware of our duty, persevering in good, and inflamed by zeal for your cause, we may, by the power of example, prayer, action and supernatural life, make ourselves every day more worthy of our holy mission, more capable of establishing and promoting among our brothers and sisters, your kingdom of justice, peace and love. Amen.

Pope Pius XII.

Prayers for Emigrants

O Jesus, in the first days of your life on earth, you were compelled to leave the land of your birth, and with Mary your loving Mother and St Joseph, to endure in Egypt the hardships and poverty of emigrants, turn your eyes in mercy upon our people who, in search of employment, are forced to leave their native land. Far away from all that is dear to them, and faced with the difficulties of a new life, they are often exposed to grave temptations and dangers to the salvation of their souls. Be, O Lord, their guide upon their way, their support in labour, their consolation in sorrow, their strength in temptation. Keep them loyal to their faith, free from sin, and faithful to all their family ties. Grant that, when this life's journey is ended, we may be all united in the blessedness of our heavenly home. Amen.

Jesus, Mary, and Joseph, protect our emigrants.

Seafarer's Prayer

I choose you today as the guardian of this ship, dear Lady, Star of the Sea. Keep it now and ever beneath the sweet light of your shining. Save it from rock, from fire, from pestilence, from storm. May your strong protection be its safeguard against the sudden destruction of torpedo and mine. Mother of him who sailed the storms of Galilee, bless and protect all who live upon this ship. Guard them from sin, dread shipwreck of souls - yet if they fail, lead them to the mercy-harbour of your Son's forgiving heart.

Kind Lady of ships, Star of the sea,
I trust my life to your sure pilotage.

A Housewife's Prayer

Be with me dear Lord, in all the things I do. Let me never lose sight of you in my daily household chores, especially when work and worry get the better of me, when I feel unappreciated and neglected, and when family troubles weigh me down. Help me to remember Lord, that all I do for my family, I am really doing for you as the head of this household.

Let my service to my family be willing and joyful, not cheerless and forced; let it be done with love in union with your own dear Mother, the perfect model of housewives for all time. Grant me a little of her patience and understanding, Lord, as I need them so much to be the means of keeping peace and harmony in our home. Let me never be too busy to hold out a helping hand to those that need it, or to stop awhile and offer sympathy to some troubled soul. Aided by your grace may our home be a reflection of your own happy home in Nazareth, and may our family be united with yours in the glory of our eternal home. Amen.

A Motorist's Prayer

Dear Lord,
Grant me a steady hand and watchful eye,
That no man will be hurt when I pass by.
Thou gavest life, and pray no act of mine
May take away or mar that gift of thine.
Shelter those, dear Lord, who bear me company
From the evils of fire and all calamity,
Teach me to use my car for others' need,
Nor miss, through love of speed,
The beauty of your world; and thus I may
With joy and courtesy go my way.
Amen.

A Televiewer's Prayer

Great God, who knew the secrets of TV before we ever dreamed that they could be,
Who loves with love divine the great and small
And dwell within the hidden soul of all,
Inspire us to understand the way
You'd have us use this miracle today.

Enable us to see in its bright hour
The magnitude of your eternal power,
And let us bless your loving majesty
That has disclosed the wonders of TV,
Nor let it ever prove to be a wedge
We drive between our souls and heaven's edge.

But let us learn instead to use it well
And make of it in homes wherein you dwell
A fount of joy, a haven of sweet rest
A common bond with those we love the best,
A means of grace, a source of sanctity
O, help us come by it more close to thee!
Catherine Curtin Fenzel

House Blessing

God bless the corners of this house,
And be the lintel blest
And bless the hearth and bless the board
And bless each place of rest;
And bless each door that opens wide
To stranger as to kin;
And bless each crystal window pane
That lets the sunlight in;
And bless the rooftree overhead
And every sturdy wall,
That peace of man, the peace of God,
The peace of love on all.

Prayer for one's Family

O Jesus, behold our family prostrate before you. Once more, we consecrate ourselves to you - our trials and joys - that our home, like yours, may ever be the shrine of peace, purity, love, labour and faith. Protect and bless all of us absent and present, living and dead.

O Mary, loving mother of Jesus - and our mother, pray to Jesus for our family, for all the families of the world, to guard the cradle of the newborn, the schools of the young and their vocations.

O Joseph, holy guardian of Jesus and Mary, assist us by your prayers in all the necessities of life. Ask of Jesus that special grace which he granted to you, to watch at the pillow of the sick and the dying, so that with Mary and with you, heaven may find our family unbroken in the Sacred Heart of Jesus.

Prayer for Friends

O Sacred Heart of Jesus, I beseech you, take under your special protection all my dear friends, whether living or dead, far or near, and in whatever state of life or occupation they may seek to serve you. O divine heart of my most loving friend, who understands so well my love for these dear friends of mine, purify it of all that is displeasing to you, and grant that I may at all times seek to further their spiritual interests. May I never be a source of scandal to any of them, but rather grant, Lord, that only the good that comes from you may reach them through me. Be with them in their hour of trial and give to them that comfort which can only be given by the friend of friends. May all we who journey together through life be reunited forever in your loving friendship eternally in Heaven. Amen.

Prayer for Enemies

If I have enemies, change their hearts towards me. I forgive them; and I beseech you, O heart of Jesus, to pardon them the evil they have done, and to draw them to follow you.

Prayer of an Engaged Couple

Lord Jesus, to teach us to love each other, you became one of us, taking as a tabernacle the body of Mary. You said: 'Be one in each other, even as I and the Father are one'. You have desired that we should live in you as with a single life, like two branches of a single vine, which your providence has entwined. Let our love pass through you that it may realize a perfect union, not only of our hearts but also of our souls; and that, growing from day to day, it may likewise increase our life in you. Help us to bring to our home enough beauty, health, thrift, strength, purity and idealism, to make it a model of the new world we wish to build with you, and to give you priests and religious perhaps, but certainly, apostles. With all this, let us never forget that it is through us that your kingdom must be established - in factories, offices, shops, in all the places we frequent, in our streets and houses - on earth as in heaven. Have pity on all those whose hearts are wounded and whose dreams are broken. Guard the promises which have been made according to your Spirit. And may your blessing soon give us to each other forever. Amen.

Prayer of the Married

Having been united in the holy bonds of sacred matrimony, we thank you, Lord, for all the favours and graces you have bestowed upon us and we humbly beseech you to make our blessed love an unfailing source of praise and service to you, a cherished purpose of peace, joy and mutual affection in our lives, a continuous comfort in the hour of trials, a pledge of our eternal and perfect union in your love in Heaven. Amen.

Prayer for Expectant Mothers

Everlasting and Almighty God, who through the operation of the Holy Spirit, prepared the body and soul of the glorious Virgin Mary, Mother of God, to be a worthy dwelling for your Son, and who, through the same Holy Spirit sanctified St John the Baptist before his birth, hear the prayer of your humble servant. I implore you, through the intercession of St Gerard, to protect me (her) in motherhood and to safeguard against the evil spirit the child which you have given me (her), that by your saving hand, it may receive holy Baptism. Grant also that, having lived as Christians on earth, we (they) may attain to everlasting joy in heaven. Through the same Christ our Lord. Amen.

For a Mother who has lost her Baby

Almighty, ever-living God, lover of holy purity, you have called this woman's child to your heavenly kingdom; Lord, let her also experience your merciful kindness. Comfort her with your love, help her to accept bravely your holy will, and so find sweetness in her sorrow. Comforted by the merits of your passion, and aided by the intercession of Mary ever Virgin, and of all the saints, may she be united at last with her child for all eternity in the kingdom of Heaven; who lives and reigns, God, forever and ever. Amen.

Prayer of Parents

O God, you have called us to be co-creators with you of these precious souls, whom you have entrusted to our care, grant that aided by your grace, we shall not fail in our sacred duty towards them. Let us always be conscious, Lord, of our tremendous responsibility in your sight, and the account which we must one day render to you of their souls. Give us the courage to go against ourselves when doing what we know to be right and necessary. Keep us from selfishness, Lord, and from being over indulgent or extremely severe with them, and grant us an understanding of their age and time, so that we can be of better guidance to them. In our anxiety for their worldly success and well-being, let us always remember, Lord, that true success can only be achieved by doing your holy will. Help us to teach them by word and example the beauty of your love, the shortness of time and the length of eternity. Bless our family by calling from it someone to your special service, and grant us the grace to be reunited with all our children in the glory of Heaven.

Amen.

In Time of Personal Sorrow

Blessed, O Lord, be your name forever; you have permitted this sorrow to come upon me. I cannot escape it, but of necessity fly to you to help me and turn it to my good. Lord, I am now in affliction. My soul is ill at ease, for I am much troubled with this present suffering. Let it please you, Lord, to deliver me; for, poor wretch that I am, what can I do without you? Your mighty hand can do all things. Give me patience, Lord, and strength and peace. Help me, my God, and I will not fear, no matter how grievously I may be afflicted. Lord, your will be done. Welcome be the will of God. Sacred Heart of Jesus, I place my trust in you.

For the Lonely

O Jesus, by the merits of the many secret sufferings you endured in your passion, have mercy on all those who must carry a hidden cross through life, who have secret sorrows which only you can know and share, and who must go on without any human comfort. By the merits of the terrible loneliness you suffer in your agony, comfort, we beseech you, those that have to bear the agonizing trial of loneliness, and make it for them a means of closer union with you. Sustain them by your

love and grace when their cross seems too heavy to bear and teach them to sanctify their sufferings by bearing them with courage and resignation for your greater honour and glory, until the day when you shall call them to your eternal presence where loneliness and sufferings shall be no more.
Amen.

For the Sick

Sweet Jesus, may your gentle hand,
bless every weary head,
Of those who lie so patiently,
in sickness on their bed.
Gentle physician of all souls,
take pity on their plight.
Oh! let your kind heart comfort them,
throughout each lonely night.
For where your wisdom deems it best,
that they may suffer pain,
Your grace shall be sufficient, Lord,
we shall not ask in vain.
O Life - O Strength - O Food divine!
Dear Lord, do you impart
Yourself to them - and keep them close
to your Most Sacred Heart.

Mildred Josephine Atherton

An Invalid's Prayer

Jesus, who as head of the Church has united your own sufferings to those of your faithful, accept this my suffering so that I may thus become an instrument of salvation and be crucified with you. I offer you the pain of this day for the conversion of the unbeliever to the light of the Gospel, and for all heretics who have strayed from your Church. Grant, O Jesus, that I may be able to carry my cross this day and always with a serene spirit, so that I may one day be glorified with you in Heaven.

Amen.

An Old Person's Prayer

Come, Lord Jesus, come and stay with me, for my day is far spent. Come when I am lonely and my spirit cries out for sympathy as a child cries out in the dark. Come, when my soul is troubled and dismayed, and the sins of my past rise up against me. But most of all, in my dying hour come, Lord Jesus: Come to forgive me before I am called to your judgment-seat.

Amen

To the Dying Jesus

My crucified Jesus, mercifully accept the prayer which I now make to you for help in the moment of my death, when, at its approach, all my senses shall fail me.

Prayer for a Happy Death

O my Lord and Saviour, support me in the hour of my death in the strong arms of your sacraments, and by the fresh fragrance of your consolations. Let the absolving words be said over me, the holy oil sign and seal me, your own Body be my food, and your Blood my sprinkling. Let your sweet mother Mary come to me, my angel whisper peace to me, your glorious saints and my own dear patrons smile on me, that in them all and through them all, I may receive the gift of perseverance, and die, as I desire to live, in your faith, in your Church, in your service and in your love. Amen.

Cardinal Newman

For the Holy Souls

Dear Lord, have compassion on all those Holy Souls who are nearest and dearest to us, now suffering in Purgatory, and by the merits of your own holy mother Mary, and St Joseph, call them soon

to their eternal home in heaven, where, by the help of your grace, we hope to be re-united with them for all eternity. Amen.
Eternal rest grant unto them, O Lord,
And let perpetual light shine on them.

A Prayer for Deceased Parents

O God, you have commanded us to honour our fathers and our mothers. In your mercy have pity on the souls of my father and mother, and forgive them their trespasses; and make me to see them again in the joy of everlasting happiness. We ask this through Christ our Lord. Amen.

For the Souls in Purgatory

O Lord, you are ever merciful and bounteous with your gifts, look down upon the suffering souls in Purgatory. Remember not their offences and negligences, but be mindful of your loving mercy, which is from all eternity. Cleanse them of their sins and fulfil their ardent desires that they may be made worthy to behold you face to face in your glory. May they soon be united with you and hear those blessed words which will call them to their heavenly home: 'Come, blessed of my Father, take possession of the kingdom prepared for you from the foundation of the world'.

For the Faithful Departed

O Jesus, by the sorrows you suffered in the agony, the scourging and the crowning with thorns, and in your crucifixion and death, have mercy on the souls in Purgatory, and especially those that are most forsaken; deliver them from the torments they endure and admit them to perfect union with you in Paradise.

Amen.

Prayer for Mourners

Dear Lord, whose gentle heart broke with love and sorrow on the Cross for us, have pity on all those who mourn. Have pity on all those whose sorrow seems too much for them to bear, who, buried in their grief, do not heed at this dark time in their lives the very close presence of your loving and understanding heart. Take the place, dear Lord, of their lost loved ones and be to them a comfort, the only true comfort that our human hearts can ever know. Let them remember, Lord, that this separation is not final, but that through your tender mercy we may all look forward to a joyful and everlasting re-union in your love in Heaven.

Amen.

To Prevent Sin

We pray you Lord, by the merits of your sacred passion and death, to prevent even one mortal sin from being committed somewhere today. Give to one soul the light to see the enormity of its error, the terrible consequences of sin, and the eternal loss it could mean without your grace. Give to that soul today the strength to turn away from the temptations of the devil, and to walk with renewed courage in the way of your love. Amen.

Prayer for the Conversion of Sinners

Lord Jesus, most merciful Saviour of the world, we beg and beseech you through your most Sacred Heart that all wandering sheep may now return to you, the Shepherd of their souls. We ask this through you, the same Lord Jesus who lives with the Father and the Holy Spirit, God for ever and ever. Amen.

Conversion or Return to Faith

Lord, you alone have power over all hearts, even the hardest and most sinful, and so we ask you to soften by your grace the hearts of those for whose conversion we pray. Give them light and strength to turn away from their present ways, and grant them the tremendous grace to return to their Father's house, before they are lost for all eternity. Amen.

For New Catholics

Dear Lord, hear this very special prayer which I offer for all my brothers and sisters whom you have been pleased to call into your Catholic Church as adults. When everything seems so strange and difficult for them, and they still feel they walk in darkness and alone, be there to help them understand, Lord, as you helped with such gentle patience the blundering Peter and doubting Thomas, give to us, who have never had to make such a big decision, the grace to understand their many difficulties, and to be of real spiritual help to them. Let us be filled with admiration and love towards those who, following the call of your grace, courageously embraced what they knew to be right, and are striving to continue with your help to walk in the path to which you have called them. Help them to persevere Lord, until the day when you will welcome them to your Father's house to enjoy the everlasting reward prepared for them.
Amen.

A simple prayer

O Lord, make me an instrument of your peace.
Where there is hatred, let me sow love;
Where there is injury, let me sow pardon;
Where there is doubt, let me sow faith;
Where there is despair, let me sow hope;
Where there is darkness, let me sow light;
Where there is sadness, let me sow joy.
O divine Master, grant that I may not so much
Seek to be consoled, as to console;
Seek to be understood, as to understand;
Seek to be loved, as to love.
For it is in giving that we receive,
It is in pardoning that we are pardoned,
It is in dying that we are born to eternal life.

St Francis of Assisi

To my Heavenly Patron

O heavenly patron, in whose name I glory, pray
ever to God for me: strengthen me in my faith;
establish me in virtue; guard me in the conflict,
that I may vanquish the foe and attain to glory
everlasting.
Amen.

To my Guardian Angel

Dear Angel, whom God has appointed to be my special guardian and protector, watch over me this day and every day of my life. Let me be mindful of your guiding presence in whatever I do. Help me to obey the promptings of God's grace and to overcome the temptations of the devil; that thus, through God's mercy, you may one day lead me into his divine presence, to enjoy the happiness of Heaven for all eternity. Amen.

Prayer for Purity

O Lord Jesus, let my mind think
as your mind thinks;
Let my ears hear as your ears hear;
Let my eyes see as your eyes see;
Let my lips move as your lips move;
Let my heart beat as your heart beats;
Let my hands move as your hands move;
Let my feet walk as your feet walk.
For you are all perfect
and I wish to be all perfect in your sight.
Only your goodness in us can make us perfect,
For you are all goodness, and we are yours.
Lead us to your love.
Amen.

Prayer for Generosity

Dearest Lord, teach me to be generous.
Teach me to serve you as you deserve,
To give and not to count the cost,
To fight and not to heed the wounds,
To toil and not to seek for rest,
To labour and not to seek reward,
Save that of feeling that I do your will.

St Ignatius

A Workday Prayer

Give me a sense of humour, Lord,
And a heart that knows no spite;
Give me a deeper vision of you,
And a love ever burning bright.

Give me a sense of proportion, Lord,
And a mind serene and bright;
Give me greater simplicity,
And love like a white-hot light.

J.H. Potter

Prayer for Our Lord's Care

I believe, O my Saviour, that you know just what
is best for me. I believe that you love me better
than I love myself, that you are all-wise in your
providence, and all-powerful in your protection.

I am as ignorant as Peter as to what is to happen to me in time to come, but I resign myself entirely to my ignorance, and thank you with all my heart that you have taken me out of my own keeping, and, instead of putting such a serious charge upon me, have bidden me put myself into your hands. I can ask nothing better than this, to be your care, not my own.

Cardinal Newman

A Prayer for Understanding

Give me an understanding heart, dear
Lord - so that I may
Be able by some thought or deed or word
To light the way
For someone who may come to me and bring
Their hopes and fears;
Help me to leave my problems for a while
And take up theirs.
So by my understanding to impart
Relief and comfort to some troubled heart.

Elsie S Campbell

Prayer for Myself

My Lord and my God, you have created me for yourself: grant that I may realise that my true happiness lies in doing your holy will. Grant, too, that I may labour unto the end for your greater honour and glory. I beseech you also to allow no one to be damaged through any word or act of mine.

Jesus, meek and humble of heart, make my heart like yours. Amen.

A Prayer of Reparation

Eternal Father, I offer you the Sacred Heart of Jesus, with all its love, all its sufferings and all its merits:

First - to expiate all the sins I have committed this day and during all my life.

Glory be to the Father, etc.

Second - to purify the good I have done badly this day and during all my life.

Glory be to the Father, etc.

Third - to provide for the good I ought to have done, and that I have neglected this day and during all my life.

Glory be to the Father, etc.

An Act of Contrition

O my God, I am heartily sorry for having failed you, who have never failed me. I have not done all that I could have done for your greater glory and for the welfare of my neighbour, for the relief of

the poor, the comfort of the sick, the consolation of the bereaved and the happiness of those who depend on me in any way and especially those with whom I live. I firmly resolve, with the help of your grace, to imitate more perfectly Christ's love of God and men.
Amen.

A Prayer for Perseverance

O Lord almighty, who permitted evil to draw good therefrom, hear our humble prayers, and grant that we may remain faithful to you until death. Grant us, also through the intercession of holy Mary, the strength ever to conform ourselves to your most holy will. Amen.

Prayer for Perfection

O God, infinite holiness, goodness and perfection, lead me to sanctity. Increase and refine my love. Turn it into a burning, leaping flame - a fiery furnace of love. Raise me above my mundane self. Do for me what I am unable to do for myself. Drown my pride, my selfishness and attachments in the abyss of the love and humility of your Sacred Heart. You are all powerful, make me a saint. Amen.

Prayer for a Journey

O almighty and merciful God, you have commissioned your angels to guide and protect us, command them to be our assiduous companions from our setting out until our return; to clothe us with their invisible protection; to keep us from all danger of collision, of fire, of explosion, of falls and bruises, and finally, having preserved us from all evil and especially from sin, to guide us to our heavenly home. Through Jesus Christ our Lord. Amen.

Bishop Dupanloup

A Holiday Prayer

O God, who after completing the wonders of creation, rested on the seventh day, I thank you for the opportunity you have given me to get away from my usual surroundings, to spend this holiday, this time, apart from daily work and worry. I ask of you dear Lord, to let my time of rest be a time of closer union with you, and help me not to lose sight of you in my pursuit of pleasure. Let me recognise you in my joy and let me see on this holiday, Lord, the beauty, power, majesty and wonder of your creation.

Let me see you in the sun and sea, snow and stars, and above all in my fellow pilgrims through life. Grant me, Lord, to lay down my cross awhile, and gather strength to take it up more willingly, when I resume my usual path through life. Let me see clearly in the fleetness of this holiday, my Lord, the shortness of time and the length of eternity. Finally, O Lord, grant me the grace of a safe journey through life to my eternal home in the glory of your kingdom. Amen.

A Prayer for those who miss Mass

Almighty and most merciful God,

You will not the death of a sinner but that he be converted and live,

Hear our prayers for those who, of their own free will,

From carelessness or indifference, or laziness

Are not here today to worship you in the holy Sacrifice of the Mass.

Grant them, we beseech you,

The light to see how empty life is without you,

A right understanding of their obligation to adore you,

And the courage to return to their Father's house.

And to us here present, O God of love and tenderness,

Grant a greater appreciation of the Mass,
And an apostolic spirit to work and pray for those
Whose hearts are restless until they find their rest
in you.
We ask this through Jesus Christ, you Son, our
Lord. Amen.

An Evening Prayer

May he support us all the day long, till the shades
lengthen and the evening comes, and the busy
world is hushed and the fever of life is over, and
our work is done. Then in his mercy may he give
us a safe lodging and a holy rest and peace at the
last.

Cardinal Newman

An Night Prayer

Stay with us, Lord, tonight. Stay to adore and
praise, and give thanks for us whilst we sleep; to
draw down mercy and grace upon the world; to
succour from earth's tabernacles the holy suffering
souls in Purgatory in their long night of weary
pain. Stay with us, to ward off the anger of God
from our crowded cities with their dens of vice,
their crimes that call to Heaven for vengeance.
Stay with us, to guard the innocent, to sustain the

tempted, to raise the fallen, to curb the power of the evil one, to prevent sin. Stay with us, to comfort the sorrowing, to bless the death-beds, to grant contrition to the dying, to receive into the arms of your mercy the thousands that this night must come before you for judgment. O Good Shepherd, stay with your sheep. Secure them against the perils that beset them. Stay, above all, with the suffering and dying. Grant us a quiet night and a perfect end. Be our merciful Shepherd to the last, that without fear we may appear before you as our judge. Amen.

For Protection during the Night

Visit, O Lord, this place, and drive far from it all snares of the enemy. May your holy angels dwell herein to keep us in peace, and may your blessing be on us always.

Prayer at Christmas

My God, you have mercifully and patiently led me through this busy year, giving more than I asked or deserved, grant me at this Christmas time, the grace of Jesus Christ. Let the gracious spirit of Jesus - the spirit of the little child as it knocks at the hearts of men - enter my life and bless it.

Let duty become touched with beauty, and justice be forgotten in love. At other times I ask that I may do my duty; today I ask that I may walk uprightly, today I pray for grace to bow myself to others' needs. Let my ears hear the cry of the needy and my heart feel the love of the unlovely. Give my hands strength not to do great things, but to do small things graciously. Let me accept kindness with humility. Heal the wound of misunderstanding, of jealousy or regret that scars my heart and let the gentler air of the dear Christmas spirit touch my life as the cold winter is touched by the gentler days of spring. As the old year ends, and the new year begins, grant me peace in my own heart; that those I love, and those I may help, may have sweet joy and rest. Amen.

An Act of Thanksgiving

Enable me, O my God, to return thanks to you as I ought for all your great blessings and favours. You have thought of me and loved me from all eternity; you have formed me out of nothing; you have redeemed me by the death of your Son and enabled me to share in the divine life of grace; you have made me a member of the Mystical Body of your Son, the Church; you have given me the opportunity of working for the building up of that Body; you have preserved me from the punishment I deserve for my sins and have given me the grace of repentance even though I have not ceased to offend you. What return, O my God, can I make for your innumerable blessings, and particularly for the favours of this day?

'I will bless the Lord at all times
His praises shall be always in my mouth'
Psalm 33.

RECOMMENDED READING

I Want to Pray But ...
John Hyde, S.J.

Praying to the Blessed Virgin
William Stephenson, S.J.

Prayers to St Joseph
William Stephenson. S.J.

Lord, Teach Me to Pray
Malachy Cullen, O.S.A.

Available form:
Messenger Publications
37 Lower Leeson Street
Dublin 2